Namaste
Blessings

I honour the spirit in you,
which is also in me.

Toni Carmine Salerno

BLUE ANGEL ®
PUBLISHING

Namaste Blessings

Published by Blue Angel Publishing
80 Glen Tower Drive, Glen Waverley,
Victoria, Australia 3150
E-mail: info@blueangelonline.com
Website: www.blueangelonline.com

Text and artwork by Toni Carmine Salerno

Blue Angel is a registered trademark of Blue Angel Gallery Pty. Ltd.

ISBN: 978-1-922573-06-3

Namaste,
derived from Sanskrit for 'Not I'.

Namaste,
used in greeting,
to show respect.

Namaste,
in devotion,
conveys veneration and adoration.

Namaste,
translates as 'I bow to you.'

Namaste,
expresses the relationship
between the Divine and the self.

Namaste,
I honour the spirit in you,
which is also in me.

In spirit, we are one.

Introduction

This book is a reminder that you are much, much more than a physical body in a material world. Within the heart, in every atom of your being, is living energy — a luminous, highly intelligent, creative essence, that exists in you and all living things. Our entire planet, the sun, moon, stars and galaxies that surround us, are all made of this essence which we refer to in a seemingly infinite variety of ways. Soul, Spirit, God, Goddess, the Universe, Universal Life Force, the Divine, Creation, Existence, Life, the Eternal, are just some of the ways we refer to this energy.

Whatever you call it, this 'energy' is what you truly are. I use the word 'what' instead of 'who' because you are more than one identifiable identity. We are all much more, and creation is so much more.

You are not your personality, achievements or perceived lack of accomplishment, your status or imaginary position in this world. That is not who anyone is. The underlying fabric of creation is an energy or force that is beyond words or understanding. And perhaps one of the best ways to experience the underlying essence of life is through silence.

In silence, direct your awareness inwards to your spiritual centre, to the divine portal at your heart, or to the clear, light-filled and infinite space in your mind. Once your awareness is in this space, you are not only connected to your true essence, you are in communion with all sentient beings, with all creation. This centred space is beyond the limitations of time and space, or more correctly outside of 'spacetime' — for in essence, space and time are one.

Let your mantra be, 'All is one.' Repeat it often. When you greet another, be mindful that they hold the same energy, the same living essence. They breathe the same breath as you. When you look at a flower, remember that this flower holds the same life force as you do. This flower is part of your soul, part of the universal soul.

Energetically, all is one. There is no separation. The biggest illusion is the idea that space separates and divides us. In actuality, it connects us all.

In a way, time is also an illusion. It seems real in the physical world, but from the soul's perspective, it is merely a way of experiencing life on Earth. We can look at time like leaves in a book. Through the pages, a tale is told, a sequence of events unfold, and for a while we become the story. But we are not the pages — we are not even the reader. We sentient beings are life's expression. We are the soul of creation, experiencing and partaking in the amazing mystical mystery of life.

Namaste, my dear friends. Never forget who you are. Never forget that we are all part of one divine creation. Blessings.

Namaste Blessing

The Divine in me
acknowledges the Divine in you.

I bow to you and honour your inner light
of pure and unconditional love.

Eternal peace be with you.

Eternal love be with you.

Eternal joy be with you
through this serendipitous blessing.

Namaste.

AUM Shanti
Peace Blessing

AUM Shanti.
Blessed are you
with everlasting peace —
beyond words or understanding.

Blessed are you
with tranquillity and bliss.
Blessed are you
with a clarity that reveals
the beauty of your soul,
and through which
all appears as infinite.

Namaste.

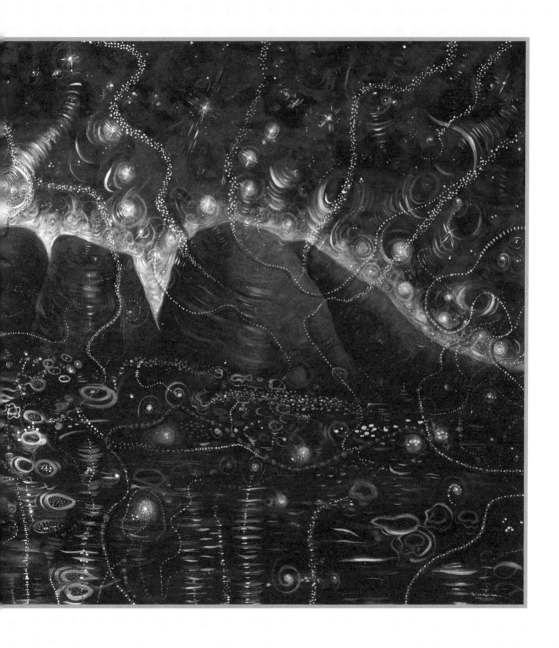

You are the Blessing

You are a blessed soul
and a blessing
to this world and others.

In giving you also receive,
for life is an ebb and flow
of love and blessings.

We are all of a single essence
and one in spirit.

To give is to bless
both yourself and others.

Namaste.

A Blessing Woven in Time

The present circumstances are guiding you
to a sacred space inside you,
from where you will see
things more clearly.

Look through the eye of the soul,
and you will find the answer.

This message is a blessing woven in time.

The time will soon come.

Namaste.

A Blessed Gift

Something beautiful
soon manifests.

Trust that all is unfolding
in the most perfect way
for you and all concerned.

Have faith and continue to hold
positive and loving thoughts.

A blessed gift is on its way.

Namaste.

A Blessing
Woven in Truth

Have the courage
to speak your truth,
and a heavy burden
will be lifted.

It is best for everyone involved
to know where they stand.

The truth will set
both you and others free.

This is a blessing
for all concerned,
but most of all for you,
dear one.

Namaste.

16

A Blessing From your Soul

You are a beautiful soul full of infinite wisdom —
stop judging and start loving yourself.

You are blessed with endless potential and are now on the verge
of transforming into the radiant being that is your true essence.

Shine your light and allow this blessing into your heart.

Namaste.

A Blessing from the Light

You are dearly loved,
more than you can
possibly imagine,
and you are never alone.

A universe of love and light
surrounds you and
showers you with blessings
that ebb and flow
in your heart.

Namaste.

A Blessed Time

The path is clear, and all obstacles have vanished.

Your time of waiting is over, so proceed with confidence.

The challenges you have faced were essential,
for there is a perfect time for everything.

Now is your perfect time to be blessed by the Universe.

Namaste.

A Blessing of Gratitude

Be grateful for all your experiences,
for all in life serves a purpose.

There is a blessing in all that did or didn't happen.

There is a blessing unfolding this very moment.

Listen to your heart and follow its wisdom.

Be mindful,
for the journey is as important as the destination.

Namaste.

Blessings from your Soul

You are a radiant being
with many unique talents —
look with eyes of love,
and you will see this.

Feel the creative power
within you
and the blessings pouring in
as the healing light
of your soul flows
into every part of you.

Namaste.

Infinite Blessing

Blessings flow to and from you,
endlessly expanding in all directions,
filling you with the healing light
that guides you upon your blessed path.

Rainbow light flows from your heart,
creating infinite peace.

Namaste.

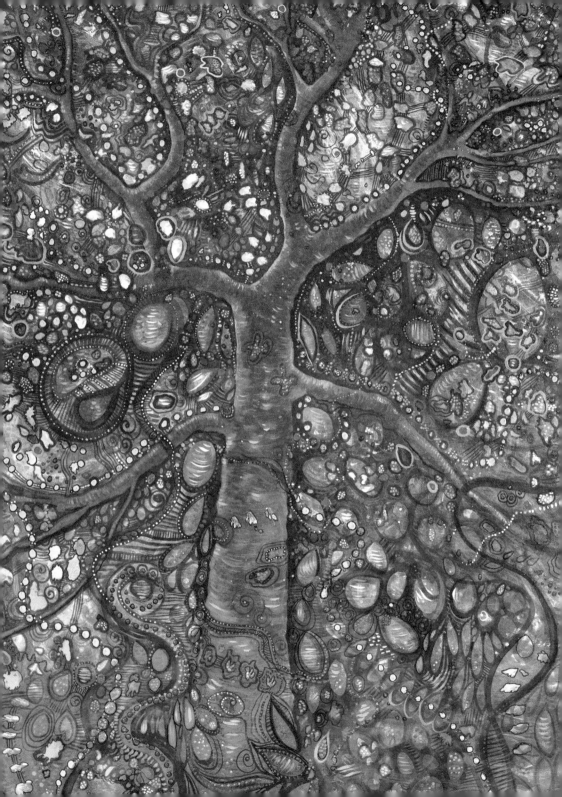

A Blessing of Acceptance

Every part of you is equally worthy of love.

Accept yourself as you are,
and this will be a blessing unto yourself and others.

If you wish to see the truth of the matter,
hold no preference,
either for or against a particular outcome.

Just be the love that you truly are.

Namaste.

A Blessed Heart

If you feel that something is missing,
look within, and you will find it.

What is your heart saying?

Your heart is the gateway to your soul,
and your soul is the eternal you.

Know that you are free,
protected and blessed.

Namaste.

The Blessing of Faith

The Universe is testing you —
will you be faithful
and true to yourself?

Be courageous,
for you are supported
by a divine ocean of love.

At this time,
you are gifted with a strong faith
that will see you through
the present challenges.

Namaste.

Blessed New Beginning

A series of serendipitous events
guide you to a renewed sense
of clarity and purpose.

Release all that no longer
serves you.

The past is behind you —
bless it and let it go.

Your life is an eternal new
beginning moving through time.

Namaste.

The Blessing of Endless Possibility

Allow your inner child to be the master
for a while and don't take things too seriously.

Have fun and explore the world
of endless possibility.

Something wonderful is created
through imagination and innocence.

Namaste.

Blessing Without Borders

In essence, we are living energy
flowing through the ocean
of human consciousness —
spiritual beings
moving through cycles
of life, birth, death and rebirth.

We are all interconnected,
and in communion with each other,
no matter how much physical space
appears to separate us.

Feel the blessed presence
of someone you love in your heart,
here in this moment.

Namaste.

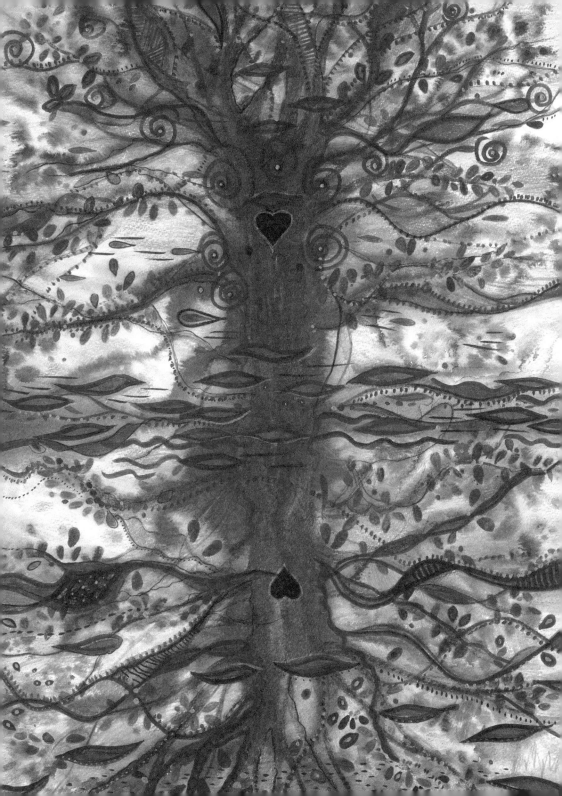

The Blessing of Letting Go

Free yourself from negative entanglements
by letting go of emotional ties,
beliefs and outdated ways of thinking
that no longer serve you.

You have the power.

That which you let go will transform
into an endless blessing.

Namaste.

Your Blessed Power

You are a field of endless possibility
with unlimited power to create.

Every atom of you is full of abstract potential
that can be moulded into any form.

Every particle of you
holds the blueprint of creation.

You are a force of nature
and a great blessing on this earth.

Namaste.

A Sea of Blessings

The Universe is a projection from within you,
and you are a projection of the Universe.

You are vast space,
and yet, you are spaceless.

You are a divine ocean of love,
a sea of blessings
and the wind of change
that flows through life.

Namaste.

The Blessed
Treasure Within

The qualities you admire in others,
you also possess.

There is a treasure within you,
and this message is here to help you
reconnect with the well of
wisdom, creativity and beauty within you.

It is time to shine your light.

Namaste.

In the land of my dreams, I dr[eamt of] you and you appear[ed] an angel from hea[ven] the earth beneath [my] feet, like a dream [with]in a dream, a fl[ower] in a flower, I won[dered] if [t]u would you [come] me to me and [fill my] heart and fill [my] life with [love]

In the begining the wind [blew] into our hearts and the [mighty] wind did howl and our [souls] were united by the love that moved the wind and by th[e] force that created love [and] [s]ome day the wind slowed [and] [m]ight down and the sky wa[s] still and blue and th[e] [s]eason changed and the [l]eaves changed colour [and] [m]y soul expanded and [I] embraced the earth [and loved you]

Sunlight Blessing

A ray of light
bursts through the cloud of uncertainty
and darkness transforms into light.

A new day is born,
and the first buds of spring appear.

You are blessed
with the birth of something new.

A fresh season of your life begins
with this very special blessing.

Namaste.

The Blessing of Creativity

Express yourself creatively
and reconnect with your inner child.

As ideas and inspirations surface,
express them without thought,
censorship or judgement.

Don't try to make sense of things —
just allow, just feel, just be.

All is possible at this time.

You are limited only
by what you think is impossible.

Namaste.

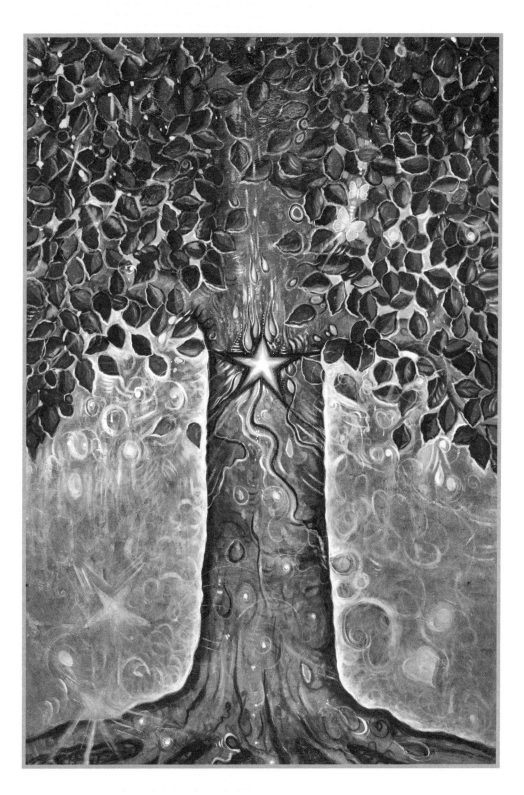

The Blessing
of Omnipresence

Breathe in light
and breathe out
any unwanted thoughts.

Dwelling on what has been,
or might have been,
serves no purpose.

Feel the omnipresent healing light
that surrounds and fills you.

Focus on the present
for it is blessed
with infinite potential.

Namaste.

A Blessing Through Emotional Upheaval

An emotional storm is forming,
and things may seem chaotic for a while.

But, as the storm subsides,
a blessing is revealed.

Respect all points of view,
for we each see the world a little differently.

Things are being shaken up
for a good reason,
and all involved will benefit.

Namaste.

The Blessing of Oneness

Bring your awareness within
and connect with the eternal you.

Love, abundance and blessings flow to you.

Feel a deep sense of peace.

Feel the oneness,
the clarity, the perfection,
and the love that you truly are.

Namaste.

'Now' is the Blessing

Life is a timeless moment
in the eternal 'Now'.

You perceive a yesterday,
today and tomorrow,
but in reality, there is only 'Now'.

Focusing on the past or future
keeps you from fully living
and receiving life's blessings.

Bring your awareness within,
and receive a timeless blessing.

Namaste.

The Blessing
of Just Being

You may have been thinking
that if you had acted
or chosen differently in the past,
things would be better now.

But in thinking this way,
you fail to see the positive effects
your past actions and choices have had
on both yourself and others.

Look closely,
and you will see many blessings.

Namaste.

You Are
Blessed Regardless

Every experience
enriches us
and those around us
in some way.

Regardless of what we do
or don't achieve,
what we do or don't do,
all is a blessing
in one form or another.

Nothing is a mistake,
for all serves
a divine purpose.

All is blessed.

Namaste.

A Blessing
in Relationship

A current relationship
is reflecting something
that is wounded inside you —
a wound from long ago,
perhaps even from a past life.

Look within,
find the part of you
that is wounded
and send it love.

All will heal,
and you will be
stronger and wiser for it.

Namaste.

The Blessing of Patience

A blessing comes disguised as a setback or delay.

This is confirmation that you are on the right path.

With patience and perseverance,
you will reach your goal.

All is accomplished in perfect time.

Namaste.

Blessing from the Divine Mother

A previously closed door now opens.

This is a blessed and fortunate time for you,
but be mindful, humble and grounded.

Feel your connection to the earth —
feel her energy and love in your heart
and know that you are eternally blessed
by the Divine Mother.

Namaste.

Blessed Tranquillity

Your feelings are surfacing
in order to be healed.

Have faith
and know that you are safe.

Trust and the current waves of emotion
shall become a sea of tranquillity
full of love and blessings.

Namaste.

The Blessing of Positive Thought

Each time you notice a negative thought cross your mind,
stop and consciously replace it with a positive one.

Practise this until the pattern is broken.

You will set yourself free.

This is a blessing you give to yourself.

It will lead you to a feeling
of deep peace and contentment.

Namaste.

the spirit of love
the soul of compass.
listen to the whisper of your
what is it saying? heart.
love.
knowledge wisdom
truth, compassion, beauty

A Blessing from the Beloved

Love unfolds your wings,
and you fly high above the earth
into the realm of heaven.

Blessed by the light of her beautiful soul,
you enter the emerald heart of the Divine Mother,
which is full of eternal blessings.

Beloved,
the world is your playground
waiting to be explored.

Namaste.

Life's Blessings

Life bestows her blessing.

She is the wind of change
flowing through you now.

This 'change' is your blessing.

Don't try to hold on,
no matter how unsettling it may seem,
for all will magically transform
when the time is right.

When you look back,
you will see only love.

Namaste.

Blessing of Good Fortune

Rich and rewarding experiences
bring you increased spiritual awareness
at this time.

Good fortune flows to you
as your third eye opens.

You are inspired,
feeling totally at peace.

Life is a beautiful tapestry
woven in threads of love.

Namaste.

A Blessed Idea

An idea manifests
endless blessings,
but you must act
to bring the idea to life.

The time is right.

Know that the world is full
of ideas floating around
aimlessly until someone
notices and breathes life
into them.

This is your time
to shine.

Have faith.

Namaste.

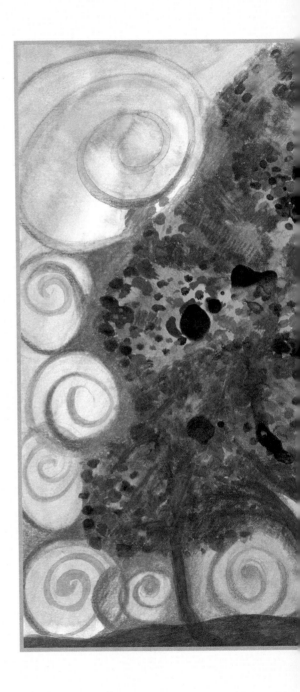

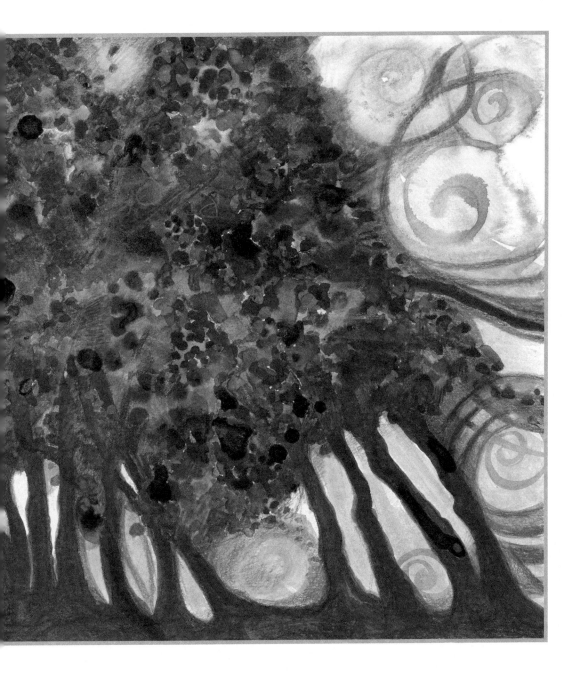

A Crystal Clear Blessing

You are soon blessed
with great clarity.

Your destiny is calling,
and your soul is shining
its infinite wisdom.

You are blessed,
protected and guided
in all you do
from this moment forward.

Namaste.

The Blessing of Questioning

Examine and identify any belief
that stems from irrational fear.

Ask yourself,
"Do I still need this?"

If the answer is no,
then replace it with
a trusting, more loving belief.

Blessings flow to you
as soon as you do this.

Set yourself free.

Namaste.

A Blessed Season

Each season of your life
is a gathering of
precious moments.

Each one has its purpose,
unique beauty, challenges
and blessings.

Everything is always
unfolding in accord with
the divine will of your soul.

All is a blessing
and forever blessed.

Namaste.

The Blessing of Meditation

Your window of perception is cleansed,
and for a moment,
you see 'life' as it truly is —
infinite and eternal.

Meditation will help you rise
above any situation and event
and see things more clearly.

What usually seems chaotic and disorderly
can be the opposite.

Know there is divine order in your life.

Namaste.

The Blessing
of a Door Closing

One moment
nothing is happening,
then everything seems
to happen at once.

A door soon closes,
but before you know it,
another opens.

You walk through
into a bright new life,
one in which you can be
who you truly are.

Namaste.

The Wheel of Life

Let us collectively, close our eyes, calm our thoughts,
move our awareness to a peaceful place
beyond all the noise, news, and drama.

Forget about conspiracies and the latest numbers,
take a moment to just be, breathe and let go.

Let us collectively remember
to practice loving kindness,
to cultivate compassion
for each other,
and all sentient beings.

Let us remember,
that we are co-creators of our collective reality.
Let's start a revolution,
of calm stillness,
of gentle humanity.

Let us unite instead of divide,
celebrate our differences,
welcome diversity, of ideas, beliefs and thought.

Let us cultivate goodwill
and respect all opinions.
It's okay to have other views.

Let us view the past and our ancestors
with compassion,
from the viewpoint that
we are ourselves far from perfect.
We all make mistakes; every generation does.
In hindsight, it's easy to think
we could have done better.

In every generation,
there are those who work to make things better.
Sometimes better, turns out to be not so good,
despite the best intentions.

Time is linear, yet life is circular, and everything repeats.
We can learn from our mistakes, but often the lesson is forgotten,
as the wheel of life turns and generations come and go.

I once wished the world would change,
when it did, a part of me secretly wished it hadn't.

Many of us spend the first half of our lives fanning flames
and the second half trying to extinguish them.

All the while, life goes on and
a little flame keeps glowing, softly flickering,
with an uneasy feeling, a little unsure when it might blow out.

All the while the sun shines, clouds drift by,
trees watch the stars at night, happy and grateful
to be part of this amazing, mysterious web of life.

All the while, the moon and stars, beam silvery light to the earth
and pierce the hearts of all sentient beings, while they sleep.

All the while time goes by,
new souls are born from old,
just as new wisdom is born of old.

We appear on this earth,
we love, we hate, we fight, we build, we destroy,
... if one is fortunate, they might ignite
a flame in another's heart.

Let us remember,
that we are on this earth for only a short while.
Be grateful for this moment, every moment.
Be grateful for this miracle we call life.

We have no real idea why we are here,
where we came from, or where we are going.

Then again,
perhaps we don't go anywhere,
perhaps we never came or left,
perhaps there is no coming or going.

Perhaps all that happens is that we change form,
from spirit into matter and matter into spirit
as the wheel of life turns.

About the
Artist & Author

Toni Carmine Salerno is an
artist and author who creates
intuitive, spontaneous works of
love. Find out more about him
and his work by visiting
www.tonicarminesalerno.com
or www.blueangelonline.com.

For more information on this
or any Blue Angel Publishing® release,
please visit our website at:

www.blueangelonline.com